Contents

INTRODUCTION

"... That whenever any Form of Government becomes destructive of these ends, it is the right of the people to alter or to abolish it, and to institute new Government,.." - American Declaration of Independence

The Government of Nigeria's corruption, failure to provide services, and inability to combat crime is notorious. These factors combined with a strong extremist Islamic surge in the region have created a situation ripe for exploitation. Boko Haram is the third Islamic militant group to arise in Northeast Nigeria as the inheritor of the voice of dissent in this fragile country, hoping to split the predominantly Muslim North from the Christian South. Boko Haram has steadily increased its attacks on the government and has seen an equal escalation in response. Boko Haram's disorganization, geographic isolation, and poor training impede its ability to achieve its objective. Having too quickly elevated the fray into an existential threat to the Government, Boko Haram needs to create a better plan. Boko Haram should combine its ideological fervor with three principal lines of effort to seize the support of the people, the mutual center of gravity for both belligerents. Boko Haram should improve its guerrilla force by recruiting, organizing, and developing along a clear path toward effective insurgent operations, not just terrorist actions. Simultaneously it should pursue legitimization from the perspective of the people and the international community through manipulation of existing democratic institutions and information operations. Finally, it should separate the governed from the government by the use of violence, providing services, and further information operations. The failure of the Nigerian Government to uphold its social contract presents Boko Haram with the opportunity to restore the rule of law by establishing an Islamic State using a campaign plan based upon dividing the government from the people, pursuit of political legitimization, and establishment of a disciplined guerrilla force.

This paper will answer the above thesis by first presenting a counter argument. The author will then present three lines of effort that are mutually supporting toward achieving Boko Haram's objective. Each line of effort has elements that are either extant or possible but still not coherently combined to achieve a successful insurgency campaign. The paper will summarize and present the key indicators that the Government of Nigeria should look for as evidence that Boko Haram is pursuing this course of action. Since the author posits that this is a "most dangerous course of action," then these indications and warnings could lead to the development of a branch plan developed during the war-gaming phase for the Naval War College's Capstone Exercise on Nigeria.

COUNTER-ARGUMENT

The counter argument exists that Boko Haram lacks the education, leadership, and training to devise a successful insurgency campaign plan against the Government.[1] Its actions, certainly violent, do not always seem to have coherence other than an outward expression of its rage. Boko Haram's attacks are criminal disturbances and not reflective of a wide spread dissatisfaction with the government.[2] The Government's allowance of Sharia to deal with family law has been sufficient compromise to satisfy the Muslim North. Further arguments are that Boko Haram is too extreme to hijack the narrative and convince people to establish an Islamic State. Finally, the Government has proven itself ready to bring a Joint Task Force to bear, fearless of using lethal force to wipe out Boko Haram, even if it cuts too deep.[3]

Nigerians are not supportive of Boko Haram. Violent tactics and separatist efforts are contrary to the hope that most Nigerians have that they can succeed in forming a lasting country. The government's willingness to deal with similar issues such as the Movement for the Emancipation of the Niger Delta (MEND) or Biafra challenge demonstrates its ability to weather similar storms.[4] While Nigeria's police force is ineffective, its military is not and can easily handle the rebels. Nigeria further enjoys support from the international community, including the United States.[5] These factors all combine to make a difficult situation for Boko Haram to overcome alone, but the wave of Islamic unrest in the continent brings allies that can tip scales in favor of Boko Haram.

RECRUIT YOUR SPIES, KILLERS, TRAINERS, AND SUPPLIERS

Boko Haram under its current leader, Abubakar Shekau, has a strong ideology while using a decentralized cell-type structure. While this has advantages to protect the force, development a more effective insurgency organization should be one of Boko Haram's top priorities, as it will help it achieve its other lines of effort. Boko Haram, while difficult to discern solely via open source academic research, appears to be evolving as it connects with Al Qaeda in the Maghreb (AQIM) and other sympathizers to help train it.[6] Its leadership should make the first priority the recruitment, organization, and development of their insurgency to help achieve their aim. This is achievable in three steps: secure resourcing, recruit into a functionally constructed organization, and develop the force.

Boko Haram's first step must be to resource itself in order to compete with an oil rich government. It cannot count on external states or actors alone though it has allegedly received substantial sums from money from an Algerian terrorist group.[7] It is also possible that it is receiving money from opposition political leaders hoping to fund instability for its own political gains.[8] The lawless conditions and drugs routes connecting South America to Europe via Nigeria are ripe for exploitation. Boko Haram should use a method similar to that employed by the FARC in Colombia to dominate the black market and thus secure the means to achieve its ends. Indeed, there is some evidence that ties are forming between the FARC and Nigerian organized crime.[9] Boko Haram has sufficient forces to seize and dominate the illicit market in Northern Nigeria; resulting in control of the established drug, oil bunkering, and money laundering links for a constant source of funds. Boko Haram can further improve its finances by utilizing the well-proven methods of kidnapping and extortion. There are indications that Boko Haram's has also recently received training in kidnapping in Algeria.[10] Once Boko Haram achieves a steady source of funding then it has the potential to see a meteoric rise much like the FARC did in the 1980-90's as it became flush with cash.

Next Boko Haram must continue to recruit from young Muslim Nigerians that are susceptible to the clarion call of vigilantism, extreme Islamic ideology, and the regional tradition of young men enforcing the laws in their localities. Nigeria has a disenfranchised youth bulge surrounded by inequities and a corrupt government rife with patronage. These grievances are long standing, and Boko Haram is the third in a line of groups that represent the rage felt in the North. This fact suggests that even with Boko Haram defeat, another movement will replace it until the government addresses the underlying causes of friction.[11] To prevent Boko Haram from falling into the same cycle, it must organize into functional lines and improve its structure. It should organize itself along the following divisions: recruiters, intelligence, local forces, strike groups, logistics, and trainers.

The creation of a dedicated recruiting force, armed with the promise of regular pay provided via Boko Haram's seizure of the black market trade, would likely help fill its ranks. Boko Haram has hamstrung itself by focusing the majority of its efforts in the Northeast, allowing the government to follow suit.[12] Changing coverage to the entire North and Muslim pockets in the South would find the willing and make attacks more viable throughout the country. The Government would have to dilute its force to react. Basic sales training found online would suffice to teach the recruiters how to convince those desperate for a vision, a full belly, and an outlet for youthful anger. Nigerians have proven themselves canny salesmen capable of scamming Americans out of millions such as with the 419 scam.[13] Boko Haram needs to use this energy. It will also have the funds to bring foreign mercenary troops to aid them, already arriving from Chad.[14]

Not all recruits are ready to pick up weapons and risk their lives. However, they can become the eyes, ears, and communications network for the intelligence division. The current cell structure works well for protection of leadership and insulates the division. Training for this role can be as straightforward as the basic "look outs." Individuals trusted over time and can receive more advance casing techniques, available via Al Qaeda training material, allowing for the production of sophisticated target packages.[15] This group can also focus upon the collection of raw material such as video footage for information operations. The intelligence gained from this group will drive the operations of the organization, such as the local forces.

The primary division to gain and maintain the support of the people should be the proposed "local forces" created in the North and every Muslim enclave throughout Nigeria. Boko Haram needs to ensure that local forces are able to execute the main effort task of gaining the support of the people and establishing a parallel government. These armed and trained young men, following the African tradition of youth enforcement of local code, will become the face of justice.[16] These vigilante groups require strong leadership and daily Islamic indoctrination to counter the corrupting temptations felt by those who suddenly acquire so much power; it must juxtapose with the government. By enforcing Sharia law, fighting government corruption, and helping people settle disputes, it can begin local level legitimization. It should directly combat all other criminal elements, other than those under its control, to provide a sense of security to the people and ensure profits. The objective will be to become the shadow government at the local level. Current village elders/mavens willing to comply and become the leadership for these forces will be the preferred option, even if under duress. Local forces can intimidate or eliminate any recalcitrant local leaders, clerics, or opponents to its dominance. By necessity, there must be a group to keep these vigilantes in line while conducting direct attacks against the Government and Christian groups.

Strike groups should consist of the most trusted and trained individuals of Boko Haram. Already Boko Haram seems to have training camps in Chad, and elsewhere, as it accesses the extensive knowledge of other militias and insurgents currently roaming North Africa.[17] Its purpose will be to execute the direct authority of the top leadership and will be mobile vice territorially focused local element. Its first function will be to keep the vigilante forces on track and punish it for any deviations from the objective. Strike groups establish control, put new leadership in place, and enable local forces. Regular inspection of local activities will be a staple function. Strike groups should eliminate government officials proving too effective. It should use intelligence to select tactical, operational, and strategically decisive targets for attack countrywide. The goal will be to raise the level of insecurity to a point where the government and Christians over react with similar violence in order to create an unstable environment for investment.[18]

Current Boko Haram focus upon operations in the Northeast, with some notable exceptions, has allowed the Government to focus military and police power there. Strike groups must spread the fight country wide to dilute the government's ability to concentrate. Strike groups will target uncooperative international agencies to remove its support to governmental efforts. Its tactics will focus from assassination, IED attacks, to larger operations such as those seen like its jailbreaks and direct attacks on police outposts.[19] The eventual end state would be strike groups capable of decisive operations against military units. This capability will require a robust logistics capability.

As Boko Haram realizes success in the takeover of the illicit market, it will have to transition the most talented of its ranks to use this underground trade as the backbone for its logistics organization. The logisticians will be responsible for sustaining the force and can take advantage of the weaponry windfall available from the collapse of the Libyan regime.[20] Nigerians have shown a propensity for navigating the complicated logistics process to moving illicit material from South America to Europe, and thus can grasp the means to provide for the whole force. The permeable nature of the Northern border and the overall weak governance of the GON should permit unimpeded efforts.[21]

The final division of Boko Haram will be a training cadre to develop the rest of the force. While open source reports do not paint a full picture, a reasonable deduction is that the connection with Al Qaeda in the Maghreb is valid and admitted to by Boko Haram's own spokesman, Abu Qaqa.[22] This access to training and education is a potential decisive point in Boko Haram's existence. Its successful attack on the UN compound and other spectacular attacks beyond its normal operations suggest a sudden proficiency. This emergence into a more capable force so quickly suggests a strong training and advisory effort. A logical step further would see the development of a training cadre perhaps stationed outside the country in areas free of any governmental control in Chad or Mali, and probably exists now.[23] Boko Haram needs to use its resources to hire those willing to sell their knowledge. There are reports that Boko Haram has hired mercenaries to help them, further indicating it has the resources to pay for it. The FARC's current plight and diminishing force would probably make some individuals receptive to personal gain while using their expertise in the drug trade, logistics, and explosives.[24]

The sophistication and intensity of attacks in 2012 reveals a thorough training effort. July 2012 saw attacks on three Christian Churches, hit near simultaneously, and resulted in massive counter riots. Trainers, capitalizing on ripe conditions, are creating a dedicated force to follow through on acts of extreme violence. The aspect of steady pay, opportunities for promotion, and a sense of belonging are powerful tools. The trainers are likely using the common rituals found in militaries worldwide combined with a Hausa and Islamic flavor that will illicit the response desired. The opportunity to create a fervent fighting force is proportional to the desperation felt by the disenfranchised.[25]

Success in creating a recruiting process that feeds directly into a functionally aligned organization would make all subsequent lines of effort by Boko Haram possible. This hinges upon the success of securing a source of funding via various means but none as potentially lucrative as the illicit market. If Boko Haram can achieve the same pervasive control of the drug market that the FARC achieved in Colombia, the Government of Nigeria will likely fail as it lacks the more robust and established democratic tradition of Colombia. A well organized insurgency will almost certainly enjoy greater success than a disorganized one as long as its focused upon the other proper lines of effort that aim squarely at the center of gravity; the people.

WE SEEK THE FREEDOM OF SELF DETERMINATION

A concerted effort by Boko Haram to establish legitimacy at the local, national, and international level could prove devastating to the Government of Nigeria. Nigeria's borders, drawn on British parchment, disregarded the people those lines would effect. Nigeria's unity is due to the inertia started by the Colonial government, the subsequent government's desire to maintain power, and the country's desire to prove its ability to rise above its own backwardness.[26] The Hausa people, formerly under the Sokoto

Caliphate, feel the damage of colonialism keenly and Boko Haram must capitalize upon this sentiment by seeking a means to change and dominate the narrative. To balance the negative perceptions that come with its extremist Islamic moniker it needs to form a political arm, tap into international sensitivity to race, colonial history, and human rights. Boko Haram is currently allowing others to define it when it could gain the strategic communications high ground. Boko Haram should create a political arm to manipulate the media, NGO's, and existing democratic institutions to establish perceived legitimization via information operations in order to create a viable alternative for the people and isolate the GON both domestically and internationally.

Boko Haram needs to establish a political arm or co-opt an existing political group to champion its cause. The recent arrest of a Boko Haram leader at the house of Senator is potential proof of this symbiotic union.[27] A political apparatus similar to what the Irish Republican Army (IRA) or Palestinian Liberation Organization (PLO) created has proven the utility of having representatives "free" of the criminality of the organization. This political arm should have three primary goals to become the voice of the people of the North. It must use the current democratic institutions to gain increased representation, engage the international community, and become the arm that coordinates Boko Haram's information operations.

A political arm of Boko Haram can ensure an increased subversive presence within government by utilizing the vote. Boko Haram must tie all the elements of its campaign plan into a single synergistic effort to secure enough votes to become a serious threat to the government. Enough votes mean that it can create a significant obstacle to the functioning of the government. Once ensconced within legitimate

10

governmental institutions its access to legitimate forms of media and international actors increases significantly. Further, if Boko Haram can graft its political arm to the narrative of the reestablishing the Sokoto Caliphate then that concept could be the battle cry that brings the North together.[28]

Creating a binding connection with Sokoto would require well-reasoned and direct negotiations between the political arm and the Sultan of Sokoto. It is unlikely that the current Sultan, also the President of the Jama'atu Nasril Islam, would find a direct union with Boko Haram palatable, but an accord with a political party could perhaps be feasible.[29] Boko Haram would be the shadow actor in a powerful triumvirate that the Government would struggle to counter. A merging would be a decisive point allowing Boko Haram to seize the information initiative and permit the political party to begin a strategic communications operation. Failing this arrangement Boko seems to be opting for an option to split the power away from Sokoto and create a religious authority in the state of Yobe.[30] While this may be more problematic, it could also serve the general purpose of moving toward legitimizing its cause, at least in its own religious context.

Boko Haram has failed to use the power of modern media to create the pervasive narrative that could galvanize support for it. Anti- western beliefs may be leading to its clumsy propaganda machine. However, if the political party takes on this aspect of the campaign it would more naturally fit into a political modus operandi. The strategic message that the party must broadcast is that the North's true government was originally the Sokoto Caliphate and that the British neutralized it. The message must be clear that the current Government is but a corrupt inheritor of that British colonial tradition. Boko Haram's members in every interview or interrogation suggest that it has a firm ideology and knows its objectives but are failing to dominate the narrative.[31]

Fortunately, for Boko Haram, the government of Nigeria can easily provide the insurgency with all the ammunition it needs to win an information operation. The rampant corruption present within in the government combined with its ready disregard for human rights is ripe for exploitation. Every field element of Boko Haram needs to be equipped with digital video equipment. A concerted effort made to capture everything from basic police corruption as they fleece the people to the heavy-handed reactions of the military. There is already an ample library of police and military brutality such as videos of Boko Haram "suspects" hurriedly assembled in town squares and summarily executed without any due process. The video by Al Jazeera, capturing Boko Haram's first leader Mohammed Yusuf's tortured body and his "followers" subsequent execution is the type of powerful video that can galvanize a nation.[32] Indeed this slaughter was perhaps the catalyst that has driven Boko Haram to new levels of violence and from a group of malcontents into an insurgency.[33]

The political arm should broadcast these human rights violations to every NGO, international agency, and media outlet it can reach. It can put governments like the United States in a diplomatic corner; questioning how it can help the Nigerian Government under these circumstances. The argument could show the parallels of the shortsighted U.S. policy during the 60's-80's to Latin governments fighting communists and the current U.S. efforts in support of African government's fighting Islamists. As with Latin America, the U.S. with notable exceptions ignored corruption and human rights violations. It took years and many mistakes for U.S. policy to develop into a more measured and thoughtful engagement as demonstrated in El Salvador and Colombia. Current U.S. policy does not permit the training and material support to any Latin American government that demonstrates the same blatant disregard for human rights as seen today in Nigeria. This message, properly delivered by articulate and pervasive communications, could drastically change perceptions and isolate the Nigerian government.

Boko Haram, once it achieves this change in the narrative and puts the Nigerian Government's behavior into the court of public perception will possibly disrupt the support the government currently receives from NGO's and international groups. Recently an aide for Secretary of State Clinton brought attention to the subject of "heavy handedness" after a visit to Nigeria.[34] If Boko Haram can achieve this level of coherent message, then it can pursue legal action against Nigerian leadership via the international courts, which can prove as effective as any targeted lethal strike at government's leadership. Many NGO's will feel obligated to either leave Nigeria as the government becomes increasingly ostracized or can be co-opted to achieve the aims of Boko Haram. While it may seem hard to conceive of Boko Haram ability to achieve this reversal in the narrative, the PLO found a way. Indeed, even the Libyan Islamic Fighting Group, a known ally of Al Qaeda, found itself supported by NATO airstrikes because of its success at winning the information battle.[35]

Other recent events, most notably the Arab Spring, have shown the powerful wave of latent antigovernment sentiment that only needs a spark to set it ablaze. The success in the spark catching fire was in part due to the fuel created by long years of grievance layered with the tinder of a message of discontent weaved by those smart

13

enough to use new technologies. An effort to find a legitimate political party, working within the democratic system, manipulating the international system, and stealing the narrative away from the Nigerian government will simultaneously work with the most vital part of Boko Haram's campaign, dividing the government away from its own people.

THESE ARE NOT YOUR PEOPLE

The final effort that Boko Haram must pursue along with its recruitment, reorganization, and political legitimization is to break the government away from its Muslim people, particularly in the North. Boko Haram has a proven penchant for violence but has a parochial focus and insufficient balance with other lines of effort. It risks becoming like the Shining Path in Peru whose extreme acts of violence created the desired instability but also turned the people against it. Boko Haram must challenge the government for the support of the people, the center of gravity, in two fundamental ways. It should expand its efforts to destabilize the country by using violence, preventing the government from providing services, and exacerbating ethnic and religious strife. Simultaneously it needs to provide basic services to the people using its illicit funds and work force to harmonize with its efforts at legitimization and information operations.

Boko Haram grasps the use of violence as is evident by its numerous attacks and recent escalation resulting in the implementation of widespread curfews by the government.[36] However, Boko Haram's activities tend to focus most heavily in the Northeast, which is its primary base of operation. While there are occasional attacks outside this area, this predictability is allowing the government to focus its efforts. The government's willingness to strike hard mindless of human rights or due process presents a significant threat to Boko Haram's survivability. While Boko Haram shows gradual maturation in its actions, it must spread instability to cover the whole of the Muslim North and the principal cities around the country to diffuse security forces.

Attacks such as prison breaks, Christian massacres, and the bombed the UN building are creating the exact conditions that Boko Haram desires. Continuation of such attacks illicit two critical reactions. Attacks on Christian targets invite retaliation to escalate religious strife. Boko hopes to draw retaliation in an effort to sow strife as reported by Ahmad Salkida, a journalist with access to Boko Haram.[37] Second, continued assaults on police, military, and international actors invariably draws swift and brutal responses by the government. These violent reactions usually directed onto innocent people will help drive a wedge between Muslims and the government.

Boko Haram must use this violence to elevate its narrative beyond terrorist attacks. It must become a patriot's tune for a return to a better time under the Caliphate. Carefully planned and successful ambushes of governmental forces will further cause police and military to concentrate for protection, making it more difficult for it to canvass the community effectively. This is where the importance of Boko Haram dominating the illicit market and effective mobilization of its workforce will come in greatest use, turning that money into services for the people. Failure to do this makes its violence nothing more than base criminality.

Boko Haram must juxtapose its violence and conflict with the state by being the sole actor that provides for the welfare of the North. A grievance of the North is that

15

revenue generated by the state has disproportionally benefited the Christian South. Boko Haram needs to use the well-tested and proven technique, used by other criminal and insurgent groups in the past, of providing services that the government fails to provide. Surprisingly Boko Haram appears to ignore this critical function of winning the people over with perhaps the exception of some basic religious schooling.[38] It needs to provide sustenance, fuel, infrastructure, conflict resolution, and fair loans. Boko Haram must balance its violent actions with a balanced alternative so that it represents a better future for Nigeria. The actions at the local level must correspond with its message for a Sokoto Caliphate and Islamic rule that will improve life once it separates from Nigeria proper.

This powerful tool can swell ranks and win the support of the people but requires significant resources. As mentioned before, if Boko Haram properly organizes, it can secure the resources to achieve what the government is responsible to provide. Boko Haram's greatest challenge will be to maintain its focus and not become enamored with the wealth that it seizes. Its leader, Shekau, is intelligent, possesses a photographic memory, and maintains a religious zeal that makes him perfect to maintain focus despite the allure of wealth.[39] The religious rigor provided by extremist Islam and Boko Haram's leadership could provide the discipline to balance Nigeria's common tendency toward patronage and corruption.[40]

The government's poor record on education is Boko Haram's greatest service opportunity.[41] Via its dominance of the illicit trade, it can generate the revenue to build and run the schools that will educate the majority of the children of the North. If Boko Haram fails to win an immediate victory, it can still sow the seeds for long-term success,

16

especially with the youth bulge currently experienced in Nigeria.[42] Indoctrination of young Nigerians across the North will equip Boko Haram with a source of new recruits. The government will find itself hard-pressed to regain the strategic communications high ground.

CONCLUSION

Boko Haram is the symptom of the endemic failure of the Government of Nigeria to address grievances, particularly in the North of Nigeria. The differences in ethnicity, culture, religion, and wealth have combined to create a volatile mix. The Government's rampant corruption and inability to manage its resources effectively is synonymous with many of the classic causes that foment the seeds of unrest. Boko Haram is seizing upon the wave of Islamic discontent in Africa as a catalyst to challenge the government and attempt to achieve a separation of the Muslim North away from Nigeria. The surge and sophistication in violence is a possible result of a linking up with Al Qaeda in the Maghreb. Boko Haram is emerging into a fully capable insurgency capable of seizing a significant part of the illicit market. These funds will allow it the power to organize, recruit, and develop into a more coherent force. It is aligning, or already has, to political parties as it seeks some level of legitimacy. If it learns the lessons of the information operations executed by its Libyan compatriots to the North, it can seize upon an effort to discredit and isolate the Government of Nigeria. The last piece missing would be for Boko Haram to combine its destabilizing actions with simultaneous efforts to provide basic governmental services to the people. These actions could see the people of northern Nigeria shift alliance to Boko Haram and achieve consensus for succession from Nigeria.

FINAL REMARKS

If Boko Haram manages to accomplish a significant portion of the actions outlined in this campaign plan, then the Nigerian government needs to shift its current strategy. The following is a list of indicators that if observed would suggest that Boko Haram is executing or on the cusp of adopting a similar operational approach. Takeover of the illicit market sufficient to resource themselves. Hiring or seeking training to build a more effective insurgency. Organizing, establishing divisions of labor, branching out into other Muslim enclaves, and recruiting. Boko Haram creates or merges with a political party, and subsequent efforts to legitimize. It begins to pursue a significant effort in information operations, particularly in the use of the internet or other media to expose and isolate the Nigerian Government to the international community. It spreads its violent operations outside of the Northeast regularly to expand its area of operations. The single most dangerous action is if Boko Haram starts providing local people with a parallel government and basic services.

To counter the Government should secure its borders to limit insurgent's logistics and training efforts. It must start providing services to the people of the North and address their primary grievances. Finally, it must have security forces that follow the rule of law and abide by international human rights conventions.

NOTES

[1] "Channels Television - Nigeria's Award Winning Television Station", n.d., http://www.channelstv.com/home/2012/10/24/boko-haram-plans-massive-attacks-during-eid-el-kabir-jtf/.

[2] Michael Burleigh, "A Rosy View of Boko Haram, the Nigerian Islamist Terrorist Organisation | Mail Online", May 24, 2012, http://www.dailymail.co.uk/debate/article-2149317/A-rosy-view-Boko-Haram-Nigerian-Islamist-terrorist-organisation.html.

[3] James J.F. Forest, *Confronting the Terrorism of Boko Haram in Nigeria*, 12- 5 (MacDill Air Force Base: The JSOU Press, 2012), 120.

[4] Martin Meredith, *The Fate of Africa* (New York: PublicAffairs, 2005), 201–205.

[5] Abiodun Oluwarotimi, "Leadership: Ban Ki-Moon Seeks War Against Organised Crime in Nigeria", February 23, 2012, http://leadership.ng/nga/articles/17138/2012/02/23/ban_ki-moon_seeks_war_against_organized_crime_nigeria.html.

[6] Onuoha Emeaba, "The Nigerian Post: Shekau... Nigeria's Most Wanted Fugitive", May 25, 2012, http://thenigerianpost.blogspot.com/2012/05/shekau-nigerias-most-wanted-fugitive.html.

[7] Emmanuel Ogala, "Boko Haram Gets N40million Donation From Algeria-PREMIUM TIMES | Sahara Reporters", May 13, 2012, http://saharareporters.com/news-page/boko-haram-gets-n40million-donation-algeria-premium-times.

[8] Forest, *Confronting the Terrorism of Boko Haram in Nigeria*, 80.

[9] Douglas Farah, *Transnational Organized Crime, Terrorism, and Criminalized States in Latin America: An Emerging Tier-One National Security Priority* (Carlisle Barracks, PA: U.S. Army War College Strategic Studies Institute, 2012), 10.

[10] Ogala, "Boko Haram Gets N40million Donation From Algeria-PREMIUM TIMES | Sahara Reporters."

[11] Forest, *Confronting the Terrorism of Boko Haram in Nigeria*, 82.

[12] Korva Coleman, "Nigeria Arrests Alleged Mercenaries In Kano Bombing Investigation : The Two-Way : NPR", January 26, 2012, http://www.npr.org/blogs/thetwo-way/2012/01/26/145932033/nigeria-arrests-alleged-mercenaries-in-kano-bombing-investigation.

[13] Thomas Roche, "Diamond Smuggling, Nigeria's 419 Scam and South Africa's Post-Apartheid Organized Crime Problem | Techyum ::", April 14, 2012, http://techyum.com/2012/04/diamonds-419-and-south-africa/.

[14] Coleman, "Nigeria Arrests Alleged Mercenaries In Kano Bombing Investigation : The Two-Way : NPR."

[15] JMO Department, "2011 Libyan Revolution Case Study" (Naval War College, August 2012).

[16] David Pratten, Atreyee Sen, and editors, "Singing Thieves: History and Practice in Nigerian Popular Justice," in *Global Vigilantes* (New York: Columbia University Press, 2008), 189.

[17] Emeaba, "The Nigerian Post: Shekau... Nigeria's Most Wanted Fugitive."

[18] Chen Zhi, "Dozens Feared Killed in Northern Nigeria Explosion - Xinhua | English.news.cn", October 23, 2012, http://news.xinhuanet.com/english/world/2012-10/22/c_131922114.htm.

[19] Forest, *Confronting the Terrorism of Boko Haram in Nigeria*, 69.

[20] Sahara Reporters, "U.S. Christian Group Calls For Probe In Boko Haram Weapons Supply, Funding | OSUN DEFENDER", October 24, 2012, http://www.osundefender.org/?p=48550.

[21] Richard Lobban, "Perspective on Boko Haram" (Lecture, Naval War College, October 17, 2012).

[22] Ogala, "Boko Haram Gets N40million Donation From Algeria-PREMIUM TIMES | Sahara Reporters."

[23] Coleman, "Nigeria Arrests Alleged Mercenaries In Kano Bombing Investigation : The Two-Way : NPR."

[24] Ogala, "Boko Haram Gets N40million Donation From Algeria-PREMIUM TIMES | Sahara Reporters."

[25] Forest, *Confronting the Terrorism of Boko Haram in Nigeria*, 52.

[26] Meredith, *The Fate of Africa*, 75–78.

[27] "Matter Arising From The Arrest Of Shu'Aibu Muhammed Bama, A Boko Haram Commander In Maiduguri | OSUN DEFENDER", n.d., http://www.osundefender.org/?p=45799.

[28] Forest, *Confronting the Terrorism of Boko Haram in Nigeria*, 75.

[29] Hassan Ibrahim, "Enough Is Enough •Sultan Tells Boko Haram •Says Shedding of Blood Must Stop", May 25, 2012, http://www.tribune.com.ng/index.php/front-page-news/41483-enough-is-enough-sultan-tells-boko-haram-says-shedding-of-blood-must-stop.

[30] George Agba et al., "allAfrica.com: Nigeria: Qaqa, Sokoto - Boko Haram Plans to Tackle Sultan (Page 3 of 3)", March 8, 2012, http://allafrica.com/stories/201203080621.html?page=3.

[31] Emeaba, "The Nigerian Post: Shekau… Nigeria's Most Wanted Fugitive."

[32] Mike Hanna, "Nigeria Killings Caught on Video - Africa - Al Jazeera English", February 10, 2010, http://www.aljazeera.com/news/africa/2010/02/20102102505798741.html.

[33] John Waghelstein and Chisholm, Donald, *Analyzing Insurgency* (Newport RI: Naval War College, 2006), 8.

[34] Andrew Quinn, "Clinton Aide: Nigeria Military Alone Can't Beat Islamists | Reuters", August 9, 2012, http://www.reuters.com/article/2012/08/09/us-nigeria-clinton-idU.S.BRE87812720120809.

[35] JMO Department, "2011 Libyan Revolution Case Study."

[36] "Matter Arising From The Arrest Of Shu'Aibu Muhammed Bama, A Boko Haram Commander In Maiduguri | OSUN DEFENDER."

[37] Xan Rice, "Changing Face of Nigeria's Boko Haram," *Ft.com*, September 22, 2012, http://www.ft.com/intl/cms/s/0/9d2ab750-9ac1-11e1-9c98-00144feabdc0.html#axzz2AG7Vv7A4.

[38] Ibid.

[39] Emeaba, "The Nigerian Post: Shekau… Nigeria's Most Wanted Fugitive."

[40] Iyobosa Uwugiaren, "Why Nigerian Police Will Continue To Sleep On Duty | Leadership Newspapers", September 12, 2012, http://leadership.ng/nga/iyobosa_uwugiaren/34690/2012/09/12/why_nigerian_police_will_continue_sleep_duty.html.

[41] "Education, Unemployment and Economic Growth.pdf", n.d., 5, http://worldroom.tamu.edu/Workshops/Africa07/Nigeria/Education,%20Unemployment%20and%20Economic%20growth.pdf.

[42] "CIA - The World Factbook", n.d., https://www.cia.gov/library/publications/the-world-factbook/geos/ni.html.

BIBLIOGRAPHY

Agba, George, Chika Otuchikere, Tony Amokeodo, Brace Azubuike, and Ruth Tene. "allAfrica.com: Nigeria: Qaqa, Sokoto - Boko Haram Plans to Tackle Sultan (Page 3 of 3)", March 8, 2012. http://allafrica.com/stories/201203080621.html?page=3.

Burleigh, Michael. "A Rosy View of Boko Haram, the Nigerian Islamist Terrorist Organisation | Mail Online", May 24, 2012. http://www.dailymail.co.uk/debate/article-2149317/A-rosy-view-Boko-Haram-Nigerian-Islamist-terrorist-organisation.html.

"Channels Television - Nigeria's Award Winning Television Station", n.d. http://www.channelstv.com/home/2012/10/24/boko-haram-plans-massive-attacks-during-eid-el-kabir-jtf/.

"CIA - The World Factbook", n.d. https://www.cia.gov/library/publications/the-world-factbook/geos/ni.html.

Coleman, Korva. "Nigeria Arrests Alleged Mercenaries In Kano Bombing Investigation : The Two-Way : NPR", January 26, 2012. http://www.npr.org/blogs/thetwo-way/2012/01/26/145932033/nigeria-arrests-alleged-mercenaries-in-kano-bombing-investigation.

"Education, Unemployment and Economic Growth.pdf", n.d. http://worldroom.tamu.edu/Workshops/Africa07/Nigeria/Education,%20Unemployment%20and%20Economic%20growth.pdf.

Emeaba, Onuoha. "The Nigerian Post: Shekau… Nigeria's Most Wanted Fugitive", May 25, 2012. http://thenigerianpost.blogspot.com/2012/05/shekau-nigerias-most-wanted-fugitive.html.

Farah, Douglas. *Transnational Organized Crime, Terrorism, and Criminalized States in Latin America: An Emerging Tier-One National Security Priority*. Carlisle Barracks, PA: U.S. Army War College Strategic Studies Institute, 2012.

Forest, James J.F. *Confronting the Terrorism of Boko Haram in Nigeria*. 12- 5. MacDill Air Force Base: The JSOU Press, 2012.

Hanna, Mike. "Nigeria Killings Caught on Video - Africa - Al Jazeera English", February 10, 2010. http://www.aljazeera.com/news/africa/2010/02/20102102505798741.html.

Ibrahim, Hassan. "Enough Is Enough •Sultan Tells Boko Haram •Says Shedding of Blood Must Stop", May 25, 2012. http://www.tribune.com.ng/index.php/front-page-news/41483-enough-is-enough-sultan-tells-boko-haram-says-shedding-of-blood-must-stop.

JMO Department. "2011 Libyan Revolution Case Study". Naval War College, August 2012.

Lobban, Richard. "Perspective on Boko Haram". Lecture, Naval War College, October 17, 2012.

"Matter Arising From The Arrest Of Shu'Aibu Muhammed Bama, A Boko Haram Commander In Maiduguri | OSUN DEFENDER", n.d. http://www.osundefender.org/?p=45799.

Meredith, Martin. *The Fate of Africa*. New York: PublicAffairs, 2005.

Ogala, Emmanuel. "Boko Haram Gets N40million Donation From Algeria-PREMIUM TIMES | Sahara Reporters", May 13, 2012. http://saharareporters.com/news-page/boko-haram-gets-n40million-donation-algeria-premium-times.

Oluwarotimi, Abiodun. "Leadership: Ban Ki-Moon Seeks War Against Organised Crime in Nigeria", February 23, 2012. http://leadership.ng/nga/articles/17138/2012/02/23/ban_ki-moon_seeks_war_against_organized_crime_nigeria.html.

Pratten, David, Atreyee Sen, and editors. "Singing Thieves: History and Practice in Nigerian Popular Justice." In *Global Vigilantes*, 175–205. New York: Columbia University Press, 2008.

Quinn, Andrew. "Clinton Aide: Nigeria Military Alone Can't Beat Islamists | Reuters", August 9, 2012. http://www.reuters.com/article/2012/08/09/us-nigeria-clinton-idUSBRE87812720120809.

Reporters, Sahara. "US Christian Group Calls For Probe In Boko Haram Weapons Supply, Funding | OSUN DEFENDER", October 24, 2012. http://www.osundefender.org/?p=48550.

Rice, Xan. "Changing Face of Nigeria's Boko Haram." *Ft.com*, September 22, 2012. http://www.ft.com/intl/cms/s/0/9d2ab750-9ac1-11e1-9c98-00144feabdc0.html#axzz2AG7Vv7A4.

Roche, Thomas. "Diamond Smuggling, Nigeria's 419 Scam and South Africa's Post-Apartheid Organized Crime Problem | Techyum :", April 14, 2012. http://techyum.com/2012/04/diamonds-419-and-south-africa/.

Uwugiaren, Iyobosa. "Why Nigerian Police Will Continue To Sleep On Duty | Leadership Newspapers", September 12, 2012. http://leadership.ng/nga/iyobosa_uwugiaren/34690/2012/09/12/why_nigerian_police_will_continue_sleep_duty.html.

Waghelstein, John, and Chisholm, Donald. *Analyzing Insurgency*. Newport RI: Naval War College, 2006.

Zhi, Chen. "Dozens Feared Killed in Northern Nigeria Explosion - Xinhua | English.news.cn", October 23, 2012. http://news.xinhuanet.com/english/world/2012-10/22/c_131922114.htm.